INTO THE KALEIDOSCOPE OF VERSES

A REPERTOIRE OF POEMS

RUPALI MISTRY

This book is dedicated to my parents – Mr. Biman B. Mistry and Roma Mistry, for always inspiring me; to my relatives, who added to my wisdom; to my friends, for the endless fun and conversations; to my country - India, whose culture runs in my veins; to Mother Earth, for being my one true abode, and to the entire Universe, for enabling my dreams to manifest.

Contents

Contents

1. A Conversation with a Rose

A Conversation with a Rose

I once met a beautiful Sentimental rose.
It sought no approvals from this world
As it blossomed on a fair summer day
In a sunny rose garden in New Zealand.
With splashes of red on white velvet
Petals tucked around a yellow circle,
It garnered the rapt attention of
Countless glittering, round dew drops.
Then that evening, dark clouds gathered.
With thunder and rain, the winds battered.
While curled up near the warm fireplace,
My thoughts turned to that rose's fate.
I woke up to the gleaming morning sun,
Walked solemnly to that little rose garden,
And there was that glorious Sentimental
Poised gracefully with a few strewn petals!
While some were yet so neatly arranged
with silvery drops shining on their faces.
Our conversation took place in silence as
The rose didn't speak any other language.
"Your beauty is perfect!" I exclaimed.
"Even though the stormy winds and rain
Threatened your very existence last night,
Why do you smile, so lovely and bright?"
The rose nodded its head in the breeze.
As if contemplating the answer silently.
Then said, "The storm was unexpected, aye!
But to be your best…always…now that's life!"

2. A Tale of Water and Stone

A Tale of Water and Stone

One fine day, Water and Stone
Got into a heated argument

About who was more powerful
And couldn't reach a consensus.
So, they asked all the little birds
Flocking at the side of the river.
The birds got into a conference,
But couldn't arrive at a decision.
Then, Water suggested they ask
The sunshine in which all bask,
But Stone said the rays were biased –
They often shone on Water's surface.
With no answer yet to the question,
They went to the wise old woman,
Who lived at the edge of the village.
Yes, she was known to be like a sage.
The evening sun was almost setting
While she put down her cup of tea.
She was busy weaving flower jewelry
To be sold in the market for pennies.
Just as she put on her shoes to leave,
The two approached her, still fighting.
After hearing both of them speak,
She shook her head and said wisely,
"There are times when I have seen
Water breaking stones into pieces.
And times when water has been held
By stone dams and embankments.
So, here's the answer to your question –
The most powerful is Circumstance.
Be gone, for there's work to be done!"

With that, she left, singing a folk song.
It would seem that she had finally lit
A candle in the dark for the two misfits.
And so it was that with no argument,
The two enemies became best friends.

3. Wings

Wings

This is the story of little Louie.
A story that tells the truth truly.

One fine day, he was on a tree
Doing his bit, chomping leaves.
And suddenly, what did he spy?
His own image in a pond nearby.
A lumpy green thing with eyes,
And short legs; he was surprised.
He shook his head with dejection.
Unhappy with his pudgy reflection.
In shock, disbelief, and depression,
He was dismayed at his situation.
And when the tears had been cried,
He went back to what he did in life.
Munching leaves with all his might.
Eating, eating without knowing why.
And there were times he did stray
Towards the pond and see his image.
Repulsed he was with his ugliness.
Reviled, disgusted and so helpless.
And all he did was eat the leaves.
He did not smile, nor did he speak.
Rounder and greener became he.
Gobbling and nibbling on the tree.
Then came a moment on one day
When everything came to change.
Around himself, he spun a thread
Spinning it till he covered himself.
Alone, he stayed in the darkness.
Not knowing what days lay ahead.
Memories reshaping in his head.

His body evolving in the little bed.
Hours ticked by, followed by days.
On the branch, his cocoon swayed.
The leaves he no longer craved.
The pond forgot he ever existed.
Till an invisible force shot through
His body, and all he did was push,
Breaking the walls of the cocoon,
Emerging in the dark like the moon.
Exhausted he was, a little confused,
Suddenly aware of his form anew.
Wings on both his sides so colorful.
Spreading into a flight so beautiful.
The pride of the garden and bowers,
Sipping only on nectar from flowers,
Little Louie had come a lot farther
From his days as a pudgy caterpillar.
Oh, happiness and happiest of times
Come to those who patiently abide
And believe in all the powers divine
To reveal the true wings of their lives.

4. Whispers of the Night

Whispers of the Night

As I lay on my bed and close my eyes to sleep,
The night comes alive and whispers to me.

I hear the rustle of the trees in the cool breeze
As magical little pixies prance on their leaves.
The air is fragrant with the queen of the night
As the iridescent fairies softly hum a lullaby.
The moonbeams spread just enough light
For me to see a dream with my droopy eyes.
And then there are the insolent crickets
Who chirp away excitedly in the grassy thickets.
Their chorus stays constant with every minute
As they spy on the dance of the garden spirits.
The nocturnal merrymakings then slowly cease
As the rosy light steals across from the east.
The world rubs its eyes and stirs up on its feet
And I wait for another night to whisper to me.

5. The Last Soldier

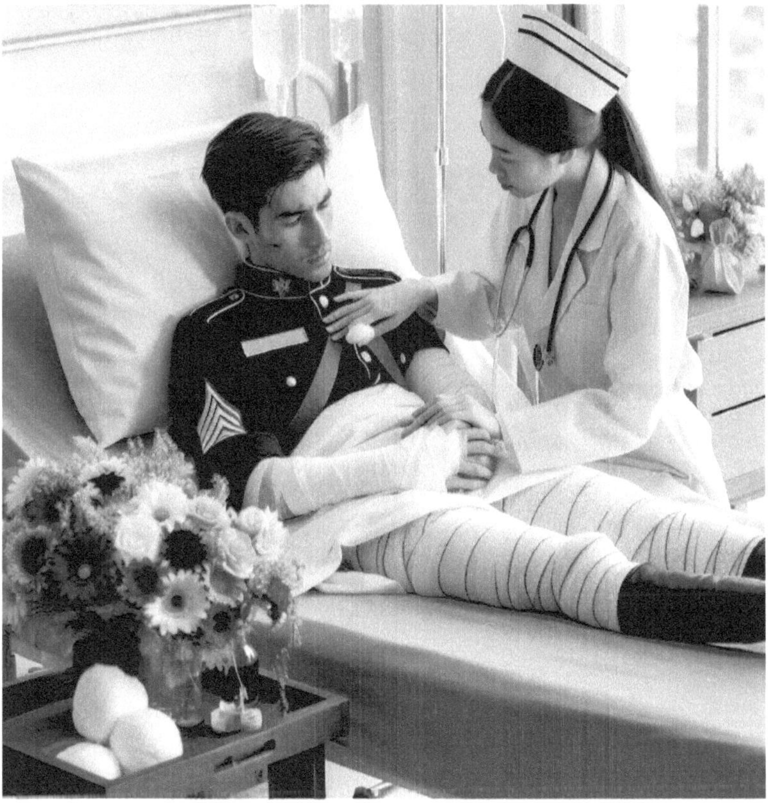

The Last Soldier

The battle was very fierce with loud and blazing guns.
The bodies of friends and foes lay fallen all around.

And when the last bullet had left the metal muzzle,
An eerie silence rose and, through the air, it wafted.
Among the lifeless soldiers, who were scattered everywhere,
There was one warrior whose breath hadn't left him yet.
Alone, he lay on the battlefield, wounded and bleeding
Unsure of whether he himself was alive and breathing.
And, as he lay in pain, the events flashing in his eyes,
He thought of his comrades who had laid down their lives.
There, he kept passing in and out of consciousness.
Even the breeze around him was still, as if it too was dead.
The last question that came in the mind of that last soldier
Was – what all of this was for – but there was no answer.
With this last thought, everything went blank finally,
And when he opened his eyes, in a hospital was he.
His leader came to him and adorned him with a medal.
And that was when he knew that they had won the battle.
To his friends, family, and duty, the soldier then returned.
Yet, that question that he had was never ever answered.

6. The Magic of Love

The Magic of Love

One beautiful rainy day,
A mischievous demigod

Threw a love potion in the air
And it mixed with the clouds.
So, the love-raindrops fell
On all who walked around,
And everyone who got wet
Forgot hate and fell in love.
The potion worked differently
For each person the rain fell on,
Changing hearts and relationships
And the way that people thought.
And so, the miserly moneylender
Smiled at those who owed loans,
And the sullen vegetable seller
Did not fight over the tomatoes.
The differences were forgotten
Of races, colors and religions.
Everyone looked at each other
With a feeling of acceptance.
And, in the evening after sunset
The people of the little town
Lit a large bonfire in the square
And around it they danced.
No one cried or complained.
They laughed and sang together.
And, all this lasted for one day.
The next day it was all over.
Then, all the Gods in the Heavens
Saw the scenes and were shocked.
They couldn't reach an agreement

On the actions of the demigod.
The people, on the other hand,
Woke up later on the next day
With memories of the experience,
And their hearts had now changed.
We all need some magical rain
Laced with this love potion
To see beyond all prejudices
And end hateful emotions.
But is a demigod who we need
For this change to come about?
Or can we each bring this effect
With the magic of our own love?

7. A Story of Courage

A Story of Courage

Once upon a long time ago,
There were three young lads —

Pain, Courage and Fear.
They found a treasure map.
The gold was in the ocean
For whoever ventured forth.
And so, they went a-hunting
In the sea on a rocking boat.
At the time to take the plunge,
Pain complained and hid away.
Fear decided to make the jump
But returned shivering and pale.
Now Courage dove in the waves
Deeper and deeper unflinchingly.
He found the treasure in a cave,
And then lived ever after happily.

8. The Old Village Road

The Old Village Road

High up the plains at the bottom of the hill,
There's a quaint little village that lies hidden.

And, in that village running right in the middle
Is an old village road used by animals and people.
On it walks the cowherd with his staff and whistle,
And the bells on the necks of his small herd tinkle.
At times, it is crossed by geese in a gaggle
Making all the big carts come to a standstill.
The road is cobbled and has tiny, loose pebbles
And in the trees lining it, the north wind swishes.
But that doesn't stop the children as they dash and giggle
With the village dogs whose tails wag and wiggle.
O the old village road holds a lot many secrets
Of the generations that in the quaint village live.
O how I long for those times when all was so simpl
When I skipped down the old village road without any reason.

9. Sugar and Me

Sugar and Me

Debuting in the greatest reality show in the universe,
I was bound by restrictions for better or for worse.

The dos and don'ts that were laid out were aplenty.
Some were stated clearly, and some, not so clearly.
But of all the conditions I was supposed to adhere,
None was as confounding as the one about sugar.
Yes, this two-faced ingredient is used in desserts.
With milk, flour, spices, fruits, and other cohorts.
It soon became a habit in a wee, gullible kid like me
As I found it to be so likable and so darn sweet.
"She's a growing child," all the people would say,
And I got away with the laddoos, candies, and cakes.
With Time, the law of cause and effect progressed,
And soon, my trueblue friend was seen as a defect.
Yes, every bit I ate stayed on with me on my waist,
And it did not take a doctor to know I was overweight.
The do now metamorphosed into a major don't
As this double-crossing thing upset my hormones.
The one that was delectable is now my enemy.
I need to break up with it both physically and mentally.
Well, the wheels of the reality show go on and on,
And I have with me now a new set of regulations.
Read this, my friends, and I hope you will be the wiser.
When it comes to eating sugar, it's best to be a miser.

10. My Midnight Journey

My Midnight Journey

Once upon a moonlit night,
When the breeze was cool

And the stars were bright,
Up, I flung a line and hook.
I caught a comet buzzing by.
I zipped past the silver moon.
She winked at me with a smile.
I went on into the dark blue
Flanked by twinkling fireflies.
I met the magical fairies, too,
With glowing unicorns as rides.
They gifted me a pair of shoes
To skip across the midnight sky.
They played a song on the lute
And bid me stop and sing awhile.
We danced to the beat of the tune
And ate our fill of moon pies.
Till I heard a bird sing, "Cuckoo."
It called out to me many times.
I rubbed my eyes, and then, I looked
At the wall-clock as it struck five.
O 'twas but a dream so beautiful.
A journey that was entirely mine.
A dream like a tiny drop of dew —
One I'd remember for a long time.

11. Incredible India

Incredible India

As the world lay in darkness millenia ago,
There emerged in the east a shining jewel.

This was my country; my India incredible
In the honor of which these words flow.
A mixing bowl of cultures and languages,
Like beads on a string are many religions
With 1.37 billion Indians calling it home,
And cuisines that are a hit across the world.
My incredible India is also a land of firsts.
Board games were created to teach morals.
It was the birthplace of Ayurveda and Yoga.
And diamonds were sourced from its earth.
My incredible India is a land of superlatives.
The world's largest sundial was built in Jaipur.
The Statue of Unity is the world's tallest statue.
And Varanasi is the world's oldest surviving city.
The more I know, the more I am in awe
Of this beautiful country where I was born.
This is my motherland; this is my home.
My incredible India makes me incredible too.

12. The Perfect Love Story

The Perfect Love Story

The king and the queen were worried.
The princess was yet to be married.

But none of the suitors were perfect.
In them, she always found a defect –
Too talkative or boring or fat or thin,
None of them, her heart, could win.
She was waiting for the ideal prince
Like in the books she'd been reading.
Until one day when with her friends,
She went to the riverside for a swim.
As they played in the cool waters,
A huge dragon appeared from nowhere.
Clutching the princess in its talons,
It flew off towards the high mountain.
The word spread around like wildfire.
The kingdom was gripped by terror,
But, one brave and fearless warrior
Took off on his horse to rescue her.
He shot an arrow at the huge dragon,
And a fierce battle then commenced.
The dragon roared and spat flames,
Yet, he was quicker and dodged them.
Finally, his sword found its mark,
And he pierced the dragon's heart.
By the light of the pale crescent moon,
He brought the princess safely home.
The kingdom celebrated and rejoiced
As the princess then made her choice.
In the glow of thousands of candles,
They both exchanged rings, and wed.
And as a new dawn broke in the skies,

With it, in the kingdom, peace arrived.
And as the story ends, I say these words —
The perfect love story exists in this world.
There's one for each and every person.
Love, like the wind, touches everything.
Just believe in it with your heart,
And welcome it with open arms.

13. Gravity and Me

Gravity and Me

One beautiful day, I was strolling down the street
With the breeze in my hair, a song on my lips,

A skip in my step and my eyes towards the sky.
Imagining shapes in the clouds floating by.
When, all of a sudden, She crept up stealthily,
And I found myself lying flat on the hard concrete
After stepping on a discarded, unheeded banana peel.
Then, there was that day, when I visited the library
Hoping to read a book and borrow another three
Debating between Robin Cook and Agatha Christie,
Or, maybe, an Isaac Asimov would be the best for me.
When, who should espy me? Yes, it was again She.
And there I was heeding to her as She called me,
As I stumbled and tumbled down ten stairs painfully.
And, I can never forget that lovely dinner party
With food so scrumptious and wine that flowed freely.
As the skies outside turned rosy with the Sun setting,
The music was turned up and everyone began dancing.
When five minutes into the prancing, whom did I meet?
Confound it! You're right – it was my "bestie"; it was She.
As I landed on the floor instead of my heeled feet.
Yes, we're in a special relationship – Gravity and me
Except, we're not like chocolate and strawberries.
I may think I can hide, but She's too good at seeking.
There's just no chance of avoiding her or escaping.
Like Fevicol, She's stuck on me permanently,
And every encounter when She shows up gleefully,
Unfortunately, ends for me distressingly – O woe is me!

14. In Search of Freedom

In Search of Freedom

In search of freedom, I consulted the vast ocean
With white-crested waves spreading into the horizon,

But it asked me to speak to the tall mountains
That limited its boundaries from all directions.
So, off I went and spoke to the mountains high.
They stood unmoving, reaching into the skies,
But the mountains said to ask the puffy clouds
That blocked them from view with their shrouds.
So, I ran on and asked the clouds floating by
They were parading in shades of grey and white,
But they all told me to question the gusty winds
Who often tossed them about to their whims.
So, I posed my query to the passing breeze
That was blowing freely among the green trees,
But it said to quiz the Sun shining blazingly,
For it's direction was determined by the orb's heat.
So, I quizzed the Sun with my squinting eyes,
As he was dazzling away like a ball of fire bright,
But he asked me to check with the Maker Himself,
For there were times when he too had to set.
So, I requested a reply from the Almighty Lord
As He sat in silence in the temple by the road.
He smiled at me kindly, and then finally, said
To ask the question to the thoughts in my head.
And, that was the moment it dawned on me
That freedom is really in what and how we think,
For those thoughts manifest into speech and actions,
And these, in turn, create societies and nations.

15. A Tale of Logic and Emotion

A Tale of Logic and Emotion

One fine day, Logic and Emotion
Couldn't decide what to do in the evening.
Logic wanted to stay at home with the book
While Emotion wanted to go for a stroll by the brook.
Logic said that the brook was too far away,
And the weatherman said it would rain anyway.
Not to mention the Sun would be setting soon.
Only a fool would walk in the dark with the Moon.
Logic added that the home had a great fireplace.
Nothing would be better than to curl up near it.
The book was engaging with three hundred pages
Of how human beings had evolved through the ages.
So, Logic said that was that, and that's how it'd be
While Emotion kept listening to the words silently.
In the end, from her eyes fell a little tear drop
And they finally ended up going for the walk.

16. The Thorns In Our Path

The Thorns in Our Path

'Tis not the roses, but the thorns in our path
That turn us into warriors by making us strong.

If you just think about it, you would understand,
There would be no heroes without the villains.
There would be no happy endings without the evil witches.
We wouldn't know success if the challenges never existed.
Yes, it's all about the way life creates a balance
To mould us all into various versions of perfection.
The thorns in our path are actually blessings.
Without them life would be endlessly boring.
There would be no wishes or prayers.
There would be no heaven or hell.
The thorns in our path may hurt or make us bleed,
But we need to accept them wholeheartedly.
Only then would we search for ways to tackle them.
Only then would we make progress in our lives again.

17. The Bee and I

The Bee and I

There's a bee in the kitchen!
O what shall I do?

There's a bee in the kitchen!
It might sting me too.
I hide behind the pans
In some kind of dance,
But the bee has got plans,
So, I don't stand a chance.
Towards me it dives
With a fighter jet's speed.
I jump to the side,
And it follows me.
Then it buzzes close –
Inches from my nose
As I hop on the floor
To get to the window.
I open the glass frames
So that it can zip outside,
But it's more than a game
For this aerial spy.
Did it think I'm a threat?
Of that I am sure,
For in the next minute,
It is all over.
There's a bee in the kitchen!
O what shall I do?
There's a bee in the kitchen!
And it has stung me too.

18. Once Upon a Lazy Day

Once Upon a Lazy Day

Just when I thought I couldn't take it anymore,
I felt a cool breeze, and … is that the boom of thunder?

Suddenly, with arms flailing, I start falling nonstop.
I see myself floating in the center of a raindrop.
Hurtling towards the emerald earth at lightning speed,
I feel a thrill moving up through my toes, and I scream.
With a splash, I land on the petal of a frangipani.
It's so fragrant and so smooth that I can slide on it.
My dress swirls round and round as I twirl in a pirouette
To the lively notes of a guitar strummed by a cricket.
In the background, I'm accompanied by butterflies
Who flutter with their colorful wings shining bright.
And as the music rises in a melodious crescendo,
Across the grey skies, there arches a rainbow.
And everything within view as far as I can see
Is bathed in a halo of the seven colors so heavenly.
The skies above then turn a flaming crimson red
As the Sun rues he wants to stay longer instead.
But, the twilight grows, and the moon tiptoes in a bonnet.
The stars cast a net of light, and the image vanishes.
I slowly open my eyes, and in my room, I am, on my little bed.
T'was but a dream, like gossamer, on a lazy day, as I overslept.

19. My Withered Rose

My Withered Rose

Somewhere in a corner of my mind,
Deep within dark caverns labyrinthine,

There lies a dusty memory in repose
Very much akin to a withered, red rose.
The petals are dry, but deeply shaded
With just a little fragrance, now faded.
And frozen in space and time, with it
Are stem, leaves and thorns complete.
In moments that are entirely my own
To that secluded chamber, I feel drawn,
And I relive precious moments of my life-
Moments that have long passed me by.
The scenes evoked are vivid and bright.
The events and people all come to life.
It is as if time stopped in its tracks
And turned around to take me back.
Hooked, I long to seek the rose again-
To revel in the walk down memory lane.
The rose lies motionless in suspension-
Withered, yet alive, by untold emotions.

20. My Mother, My Angel

My Mother, My Angel

In the small sunny balcony
That faces the western hills,

On one breezy, summer day
Mom kept some pots of clay.
In all those, she sowed seeds –
Carrom, mustard and chillies.
Then there were some more
With spinach and tomatoes.
A special pot held the Tulsi.
In two, red-rose bushes grew.
And in a few, with large leaves
Sat the ornamental varieties.
That's a lovely garden in a flat!
What more could one say to that?
But there are things more beautiful
That Mom cultivated in my soul.
The seeds of "Happiness" and "Hope"
Have grown like great green oaks.
The "Never Give Up," with strong roots
Has spread deep into my attitude.
A special rambler called "Love"
Yeilds buds redder than blood
On the spiraling stalk of "Prayer"
That shoots right up to the heavens.
While bunches of "Music" and "Wit"
Speckle the hedge of "Do Your Best."
As the keeper of this sacred garden,
She waters and prunes every day.
Wouldn't it be correct to state, then
That she's the Gateway between
The Mortal me and the Divine?

My Mother – my angel in disguise.

21. The Spring-Summer Collection

The Spring-Summer Collection

The cool breeze at dawn
Gently awakens the leaves on the trees.
The Sun rising on the horizon
Greets everything with rosy kisses.
The birds sing delightful songs
With chirps, whistles, coos, trilling and drumming.
They fly in the blue skies, or, in the trees, throng
As they serenade and welcome the morning.
The flowers bloom in a riot of colors
Dotting the green meadows and fields.
The butterflies, from cocoons, emerge
Showing off their newly painted wings.
Even the creepy crawly ones
Have their moments in the Sun.
With rustles, hums, crackles, zipping and rattling,
They all partake in the artistic presentation.
The old hills stand tall in the distance
Splashed in shades of brown and green.
Listen hard, and you may hear in their silence
Tales from last night, and their dreams.
Yes, this is indeed the grandest show.
And everyone has an invitation.
A ticket for a seat in the front row
For Nature's Spring-Summer Collection.

22. From the Witch's Chronicles

From the Witch's Chronicles

A long, lengthy time ago
There lived a king and queen.
They had a baby daughter —
The prettiest anyone had seen.
One dark night, an evil witch
Stole into the infant's room.
The bonnie baby she then picked
And flew away on her broom.
A room in a locked tower high
Was where the princess grew up,
With blonde hair and blue eyes
And no company except the evil one.
One day, a prince wandered astray
And stumbled upon the tower.
The princess let down her long tresses
So he could climb up to meet her.
The prince tried hard to ascend,
But kept falling off midway,
For he loved his cakes and croissants,
And had a lot of weight on his waist.
Finally, after many many tries,
He made it to the princess's chamber.
Huffing and puffing from the climb,
He vowed to save her from the danger.
That was when the witch arrived
And saw the prince with the princess.
The prince raised his sword to strike
But that only spiked his blood pressure.
The battle was short and one-sided.

The witch turned him into a frog.
And to add to his woeful plight,
She threw him into a muddy bog.
And so, it was that during rainy nights
One would often hear him croaking,
"O! I wish I'd eaten less and exercised,
And not slept through military training."
Well, that was how this story ended.
And I hope this helps you realize.
Good health comes from self-discipline.
Don't wait to lose it and then be wise.

23. The Reward

The Reward

Once upon a long time ago,
There lived a wealthy man.

With money, his coffers did flow,
And there was nothing he lacked.
Silken clothes, jewels and gold –
His closets were full of them.
A mansion, servants at his call,
And plates encrusted with gems.
Yes, he called himself fortunate
As he had all of life's rewards.
He felt he had all the happiness,
And that he needed nothing more.
Then, one hot day, his caravan
Stopped to rest in the afternoon.
The chariots parked under a banyan
That had vast branches and roots.
As he got down to stretch his legs,
He saw a man dressed commonly.
Who smiled benevolently at him
And asked if he was hungry or thirsty.
With disdain, the rich man denied
And told him that he had no wants.
The man bowed his head and smiled
And turned away to another person.
This man served food and water
To people who rested under the tree.
He took no money even if offered,
And this, the affluent man saw silently.
As the sun set, he questioned
That man why he did what he did.
The man smiled and invited him

To serve with him food to the needy.
The opulent man laughed loudly
And agreed just to humor him.
He served a weary traveler a meal
In a plate made of woven leaves.
All of a sudden, he was overcome
With an emotion hitherto unknown,
From his eyes, tears flowed freely, and
He felt at peace and happy all at once.
As he looked at the common man,
That man just smiled at him.
He knew that this humane action
Had turned to dust his arrogance.
As the princely man sat in the chariot,
And his caravan began to move,
He realized he had been rewarded
By his own service that afternoon.
A reward that couldn't be measured
By diamonds, gold and gemstones.
It was a prize he'd always treasure
From his generous gesture alone.
I hope that like the wealthy man,
My friends, you too realize –
An act of kindness and compassion
Is itself the true reward in our lives.

24. The Upside-Down Man

The Upside-Down Man

There once was a man
Who lived upside-down.

And people in his town
Called him a silly clown.
He walked on his hands
With his hat on his feet.
It was a funny sight as
He "strolled" in the streets.
He'd sit down to eat in a
Manner that was peculiar
With his head on the chair
And both his legs in the air.
As if this was not enough,
He spoke in a weird tongue
In which all of his words
Were backwards strung.
So, in the market, as he said,
"Lard of pound a need I!",
He ended up getting punched
And a pair of black eyes.
And there was that day too
When he asked a pretty lass,
"Please me with dance you would?"
What do you think she did next?
The girl frowned, and well,
She whacked him on his head,
And then off she quickly fled
After calling him ill-bred!!!
Then, one wet, rainy evening
While "walking" up the hill,
He slipped and came rolling

Down like the ball in skittles.
His head hit a hard rock,
And in a hospital, he woke,
But in a miracle of sorts,
He had been fully cured.
So, this is the end of the story
Of the strangest man in town.
He now makes people happy,
In the circus, as a clown.

25. Sounds of Summer

Sounds of Summer

There is no day in the entire year
As melodious as a day in summer.

Listen to the breeze in the trees
Rustling with the prancing leaves.
And in the distance, far, far away,
A koel calls out to its dear mate.
The blue sky without any spots
Provides the perfect backdrop.
The sunlight spreads as if on cue
Painting all things in a golden hue.
While boughs laden with mangoes
Shout to be picked as they hang low.
But no one is as busy as the bees
As they buzz around making honey.
The evening brings some respite
To the birds as they dash about —
Tiny larks and colored pigeons,
Mighty hawks and dark ravens.
And if you are keen-eyed, my dear,
You might even spot a kingfisher.
Their songs are heard everywhere —
A medley of tunes in the zephyrs.
Falling from this crescendo of light,
The day melts into the silent night.
I'm sure you'd agree when I say
There's no comparison for this day.
Yes, I'd trade other days of the year
To listen to the sounds of summer.

26. The Race

The Race

The tracks were set-
The runners in place-

While people watched
With bated breaths.
At the loud gunshot,
The racers were off
With fast strides to
Beat the ticking clock.
As they reached the
Last lap, all of them
Rushed ahead and sped
With all their strength.
And then it happened –
The first racer's fall –
A stumble – it seemed
Like he had lost it all.
As he hit the ground,
He felt a hand on his
Shoulder, and looked up
To see another racer
Who helped him stand
And didn't leave his side
Till they both had crossed
The white finishing-line.
Yes, the race was lost,
But he had found a friend.
And later, that day, he asked
Him, "Why did you help?"
To which his new comrade
Said, "it may seem crazy, yet
I believe – life's about helping,

And winning isn't everything."

27. The Oyster

The Oyster

A long, long time ago,
At the bottom of the sea,

There lived a little oyster
As blue as he could be.
He hardly ever spoke
And rarely ever smiled
At all the sea folks who
Used to pass him by.
"Why are you so glum?"
Said the sea anemone
"Cheer up my little one!"
As she waved gleefully
The oyster didn't smile
And one could not see
His tears as he sighed
And spoke on ruefully.
"You are so colourful
And look very pretty
With your many arms
Moving with the sea.
And the fishes there,
Just look at them go
With their bright tails
Like twirling rainbows.
While here I am all day
In my drab little shell —
Nothing to do and say,
And no stories to tell."
And so, the oyster spent
Its whole life in the sea.
And on one fine, sunny day,

It washed up on the beach.
The girl shouted happily
As she held it in her hands
And showed it to everybody
Who had gathered around.
Joy lit up her blue eyes
As they found the pearls.
They said she was lucky
To find such a big oyster-
Who was by now thinking and
Smiling at them from Heaven
"I wish I'd known all this time –
My worth- happy I'd have been."
And so, it is dear friends
As plain as truth can be.
Why fret over the reasons?
Trust in Him is all you need.

28. Marriage - A Knotty Affair

Marriage - A Knotty Affair

Some pertinent observations come to my mind
When mulling over affairs of the marriage kind.
I'm sure you too will give these some thought
To understand the implications of tying the knot.
So, at the altar, you and your would-be-better-half
Exchange vows that you'll keep for your entire life,
And it'll be some years before you begin to realize
That you should've read deeper between the lines.
The first vow – be together come what may –
Seems like fun and very easy you would say
Till the moment you start losing your space
And can't hang out anymore with your friends.
The second vow – to love each other for eternity-
Seems wonderful and gives a warm, fuzzy feeling
Till you forget to remember those very dates
Of the days you both met, got engaged and wed.
The third vow – to give your best version to the other
Seems like something you can do without any bother
Till you see there are so many times when
The best version of you just goes into hiding.
The fourth vow – to love each other's family like your own –
Seems like a thing you can already consider as done
Till you're caught in the crossfire of their differences
And can't decide whose side you should be taking.
And yet you want to hang on to that last bit of thread
In the name of loving and caring – well I'll be damned!
So, I pray that luck be on your side as you dare
To enter the world of this very knotty affair.

29. The First Wages

The First Wages

"More! More! I want some more!"
The tiny voice would've gone unheard.

I turned to meet an outstretched hand,
A scruffy face and a head full of sand.
I stared down at the beggar child.
His eyes danced; his lips smiled.
His little fingers lined with dirt
Held lightly the folds of my shirt.
'Be gone!" said I, "So unsatisfied."
The amount I'd given was justified!
Not one extra coin would I disburse
To this depraved lad, this curse!
I glared into his eyes again.
I hoped to see fear, even shame.
But my outburst had been in vain.
His beaming smile did not change.
Instead, in a voice crystal clear,
He spoke to me and I did hear.
"I'm all alone – Oh! Please, please!"
The winds and cold do not cease.
There was a time when I had known
Warm caresses – my mother's own.
And long past the twilight hours,
She'd tell me all about the stars.
She left me all alone one day,
And as she was going – did say,
""Let not the hunger and the cold
Make you beg, or sell your soul.
Look for work and you will find
In the fields – something to bind,
Or in the big, busy marketplace-

If you work hard, it will pay.
Do not fear for me, my son!
Not far from you will I be gone.
When people tell you I have died,
Look for the new star in the sky.""
And so, it's not alms that I want,
Just a little fare for the "2 Down."
No more moments I must waste
If I want a job at the marketplace.
Not more than a 2-rupee coin
For the new job I have to join!
But this you will not do for free-
Your heavy basket I shall carry."
I looked down at him again.
His eyes now held only pain.
His proud chin, turned up high,
So full of hope – this little boy.
And every word he said was true.
He was his own living proof.
Undefeated by life's miseries yet,
He was just like the black cygnet.
And, along with me he did hurry.
My blue basket, for me did carry.
"Here's the coin! Now rest a while!"
And I saw again – that beautiful smile.

30. These Times

These Times

These are the times of the Coronavirus Disease
With both love and humanity, on a tight leash.

No kissing, no hugging, no touching, please.
Make sure the hands are 20-seconds-clean.
Will they ever be clean? Will I ever be sure?
Will I ever be able to go outside like before?
Will I meet my friends and hang out in crowds?
Will this social distancing end? So many doubts!
"Stay away!" say the wise, "It will break the curse!"
"Stay indoors, or this pandemic will become worse."
Who is to blame? Does it really matter now?
This forced isolation has opened minds somehow.
We beg for forgiveness from Mother Nature's fury
While some lose the fight in a battle so lonely.
Where did the souls of so many people go?
Where is our Saviour, and where is the cure?
Some say we are paying for bad karma and sins.
Do we need more deaths for alarm bells to ring?
When will we realize the simple rule of Evolution?
We were gifted intelligence to protect Her creations.
Somewhere down that road, we got really lost,
And so, here we are now, paying that high cost.
She is furious with our recklessness, so we pray
For a cure that we may walk our streets again.
The air's clearer now; She rejoices in many ways.
In the midst of this war, did we learn anything?
Or will all this suffering and death be in vain?
A few years later, will a scourge occur again?
People – this is the word we use for ourselves.
Together we form the Collective Consciousness.
What one does affects another – this is the truth.

We need to understand this and recognize it soon.
So do not hoard – there are those who need.
The old and infirm can't move as they please.
The afflicted don't deserve this discrimination.
We depend on each other as societies and nations.
Will we win against this virus? Are we so sure?
During these times, whom do we look towards?
The Universe? God? The doctors? The nurses?
Or does the answer lie within each one of us?
Like the deadly Coronavirus, this debate rages
While the disease takes its toll in all the stages.
With time, this will pass and things will be alright.
While our hopes see us through this terrible night.

31. Listen to the Raindrops!

Listen to the Raindrops!

Listen to the raindrops as they're falling
From the grey skies on the window panes.

A chit chit chattering in the pitter pattering,
I can hear them calling out my name.
"Come outside and play," they sing loudly.
"Get your friends 'n brothers 'n sisters too.
Splashing around in the rain is exciting,
And don't forget to put on your gumboots."
Trying to catch the raindrops in our hands,
Feeling them run down our hair and faces,
Jumping in puddles of water and sand,
Shouting, we play with the frogs and snails.
Now the fire burning in the hearth is warm,
And a spot of brandy is inviting, too.
The evening skies turn cloudy and dark
While the rain is still falling on the roof.
A chit chit chattering in the pitter pattering,
Can you hear them calling out your name?
"Come outside and play," they sing loudly.
"Come outside and play…till we go away."

32. The Apostrophe and Me

The Apostrophe and Me

With the bright sun scorching
The afternoon skies at three,

I turned the page to
The Apostrophe.
Little did I know about
Grammar's sinister plot
For the apostrophe to
Put me in a tight spot.
Apparently, the apostrophe
Works just like quick concrete
Holding words together when
One or more letters are missing.
It appears in can't and in don't,
But not in pant and in font.
Wouldn't, couldn't and shouldn't
Would all be incorrect without it.
All's well so far, but it doesn't end.
For the apostrophe, with a friend – the s
Is also used to show possession –
Something belonging to someone else.
Here it gets murkier as the s
Follows it if the possesor's singular,
And if it's a plural that ends in an s,
The apostrophe alone follows that s.
So, if Larry had a cat that had a tail,
It's correct to write Larry's cat's tail.
If he had cats, there'd be many tails,
And it's written as Larry's cats' tails.
Give up already? No? there's more.
What about children, men, women,
Mice and geese – no s ends these.

Here both the apostrophe and s come in.
So, it's - children's toys, men's shoes,
And women's department all true.
Adding to all that confusion
Is that most confounding rule.
Now it's should be used as "it is".
And here's where the catch is —
It's also used with no apostrophe
As the bird's in its nest on the tree.
To apostrophe or not to apostrophe
That was the question you see.
Was it Karen's and Jane's bikes?
Or Peter and Ron's fight?
I closed the book with bleary eyes
Not certain if I had got it right
Praying to all the powers that be
To help me with the apostrophe.

33. 'Twas on a Rainy Night

'Twas on a Rainy Night

Clouds in the twilight
Hid the Sun's last rays.

Thundering gunmetal
With flashy electric trails.
Flanked with darkness,
Sudden came the rain.
Unpredictably, like tears
From eyes awash in pain.
Drops splashed all around
In the directionless breeze.
Cold, they hit the ground
Pitter pattering mindlessly.
Racing together to form
Streams of water and dirt,
Uprooting great trees from
The bowels of the earth.
As Winds cried out loudly
Making time stand still,
Night swallowed the light.
Only shadows were seen
That seemed to join in the
Dance of destruction
Orchestrated by nature
In the cycle of creation.

34. Comma Rules!

Comma Rules!

Because it would not serve any cause
For words to be read without a pause,
Here comes a mark with a superpower,
And you can call that hero – A Comma!
It is always up and ready to assist

While separating the items in a series
Like the list you'd use when you visit
A shop to get bread, milk and cheese.
Sometimes, it makes an appearance
In such a series before the conjunction.
Here, it's known as the Oxford comma
As in alpha, beta, gamma, and delta.
It springs into action in a sentence
Between clauses that are independent.
So, it would then be correct to write –
The night is dark, but the moon is bright.
It separates the main part of a sentence
From an introductory clause or phrase.
As in – when I stepped out of the door,
I tripped on my cat and fell on the floor.
If there is a phrase or clause that isn't
Important to the meaning of a sentence,
Then the helpful Comma encloses it all.
As in – Ben, the first one, had a great fall.
It jumps in to set off direct quotations
Said by the speaker in conversations.
As in – Chloe said, "I wish I could fly
Just like the birds in the blue sky."
When writing a date, it's used in a pair
To separate the year from the sentence.
As in – Years ago, on August 8, 1928,
June said "I do" to John as they wed.
If a title follows a name in a sentence,
Then it is set off by Commas in a pair.

As in – Sandra Smith, MD, will now lead
The team in the department of pathology.
And numbers greater than four digits
Are split by Commas into groups of three.
So, start from the right, and you'd write –
100,000,000,000 stars in our galaxy!!!
Now you'd think that a pause in speech
Is where the Comma is placed correctly,
But it would do you a world of good
If you remember the rules of its use.
The reason for that is simple, you see.
We all pause differently when we speak.
If you place Commas using your breath,
They'd be incorrect and make no sense.

35. The Choice

The Choice

'Twas on a glowing autumn evening,
There came at Stan's door a knocking.

Two guests sat near the hearth
The angel of life and the angel of death.
One wore robes of the finest silk
Like the sun rising over the hills.
The other was adorned in shades
Of changing leaves in the glades.
Each put forth his argument
Bidding Stan to take a decision,
For whomever he chose to be with
Would stay and the other would leave.
"Life is like a stroll through
A corridor with many doors
Behind each of which lies
A sea of possibilities."
"Death is the end
Of all suffering.
It is the place where
One rests in peace."
"Life is like a race
Through a puzzling maze
With twists and turns
Of highs and lows."
"In death lies the final
Truth that makes people
Equal for it sees no
Barriers and no emotions."
"Life is like a river flowing
Through deep valleys finding
Its way through stones and

Changing them into sand."
"Death seeks no deeds or
Accomplishments for
It will eventually come
To everything in turn."
Having heard them both,
It was Stan's turn to speak.
He said, "Death is inevitable
And will certainly overtake.
But life holds experiences
In each and every moment.
The pain and the glory
Together make the story."
So, as day came to end the night,
He held the hand of the angel of life.
And, the angel of death who said no more
Was shown out through the door.